Build-a-Skill Instant Books

Color, Shape, and Number Words

Written by
Kim Cernek

With contributions by Rozanne Lanczak Williams

Editors: Vicky Shiotsu and Stacey Faulkner
Illustrators: Jenny Campbell and Darcy Tom
Cover Illustrator: Rick Grayson
Designer: The Development Source
Art Director: Moonhee Pak
Project Director: Betsy Morris

Table of Contents

Introduction

About the Build-a-Skill Instant Books Series

The *Build-a-Skill Instant Books* series features a variety of reproducible instant books that focus on important reading and math skills covered in the primary classroom. Each instant book is easy to make, and once children become familiar with the basic formats that appear throughout the series, they will be able to make new books with little help. Children will love the unique, manipulative quality of the books and will want to read them over and over again as they gain mastery of basic learning skills!

About the Build-a-Skill Instant Books: Color, Shape, and Number Words

This book features color, shape, and number words in fun and easy-to-make instant books. Children will develop fine motor skills and practice following directions as they cut, fold, and staple the reproducible pages together to make flip books, step books, mini books, and more! As children read and reread their instant books, they will strengthen their decoding skills and increase their sight word vocabulary.

Refer to the Table of Contents to help with lesson planning. Choose instant book activities that fit with the curriculum goals in your regular or ELL classroom. Use the instant books to practice skills or introduce new ones. Directions for making the instant books appear on pages 3 and 4. These should be copied and sent along with the book patterns when assigning a bookmaking activity as homework.

Making and Using the Instant Books

Most of the instant books in this resource require only one or two pieces of paper. Copy the pages on white copy paper or card stock, or use colored paper to jazz up and vary the formats. Children will love personalizing their instant books by coloring them, adding construction paper covers, or decorating them with collage materials such as wiggly eyes, ribbon, and stickers. Customize the instant books by adding extra pages, or by creating your own Flip Book with the reproducible on page 32.

Children can make instant books as an enrichment activity when their regular classwork is done, as a learning center activity during guided reading time, or as a homework assignment. They can place completed instant books in their classroom book boxes and then read and reread the books independently or with a reading buddy. After children have had many opportunities to read their books in school, send the books home for extra skill-building practice. Encourage children to store the books in a special box that they have labeled "I Can Read Box."

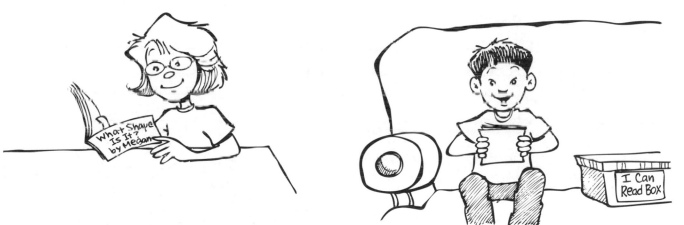

Directions for Making the Instant Books

There are five basic formats for the instant books in this guide. The directions appear below for quick and easy reference. The directions are written *to* the child, in case you would like to send the bookmaking activities home as homework. Just copy the directions and attach them to the instant book pages.

Flip Books, pages 5, 8, 13, 20, and 21

1. Finish the book by tracing the words and/or coloring the pictures.

2. Cut out the flip book and word cards.

3. Staple the word cards to the flip book.

4. "Flip up" each card to practice reading your words.

Step Book, pages 6–7, 14–15, and 22–23

1. Cut out the seven boxes.

2. Put the pages in order with the smallest square on top.

   Staple the pages at the top to make a book.

3. Write the words on the lines.

4. Draw pictures to match the words.

5. Read your book!

Mini Book, pages 18–19 and 27–28

1. Finish the book by writing the words and/or numbers.

2. Cut apart the pages.

3. Put the pages in order. Staple them on the left.

Optional: Make and decorate a construction paper cover.

Read-and-Write Book, page 11–12

1. Cut out the book and glue it to a piece of construction paper the same size.

2. Trace the color words.

3. Cut out the word cards. Staple them to the top strip.

4. Write about your favorite color on the bottom strip.

5. Fold the book in half and decorate the cover.

Optional: Staple extra writing paper to the book.

Strip Book, pages 9–10, 16–17, 24–25, 26, and 29–31

1. Finish the book by writing the words or numbers.

2. Draw any missing pictures. Color the pictures.

3. Cut out the strips.

4. Put the pages in order. Staple them on the left.

Note: For the Bug Countdown on pages 29–31:
• Trace the number words on each page.
• Draw the matching number of bugs in each picture.

Build-a-Skill Instant Books • Color, Shape, and Number Words © 2015 Creative Teaching Press

Colors Flip Book

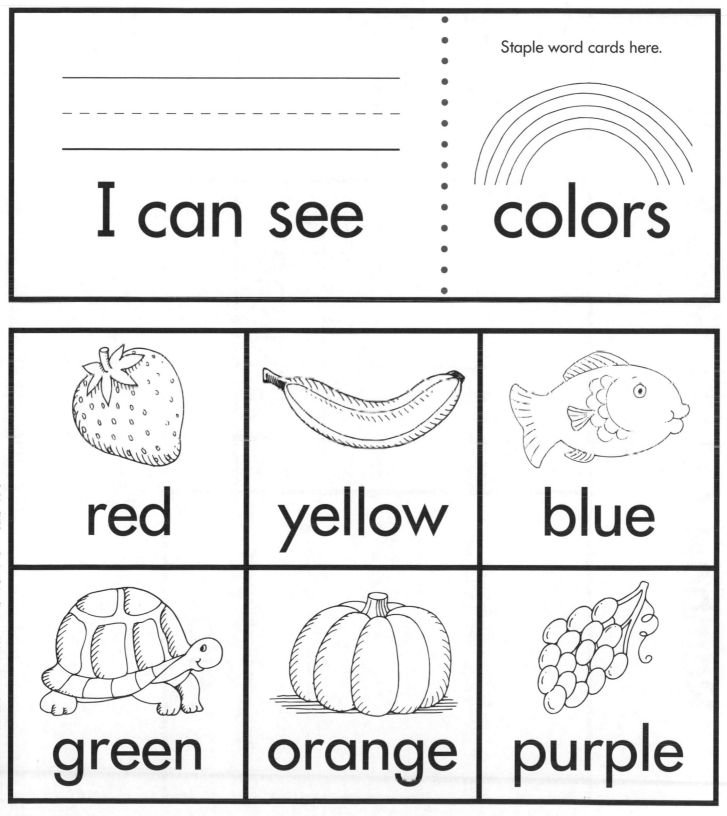

Staple word cards here.

I can see

colors

red

yellow

blue

green

orange

purple

Rainbow Colors Step Book

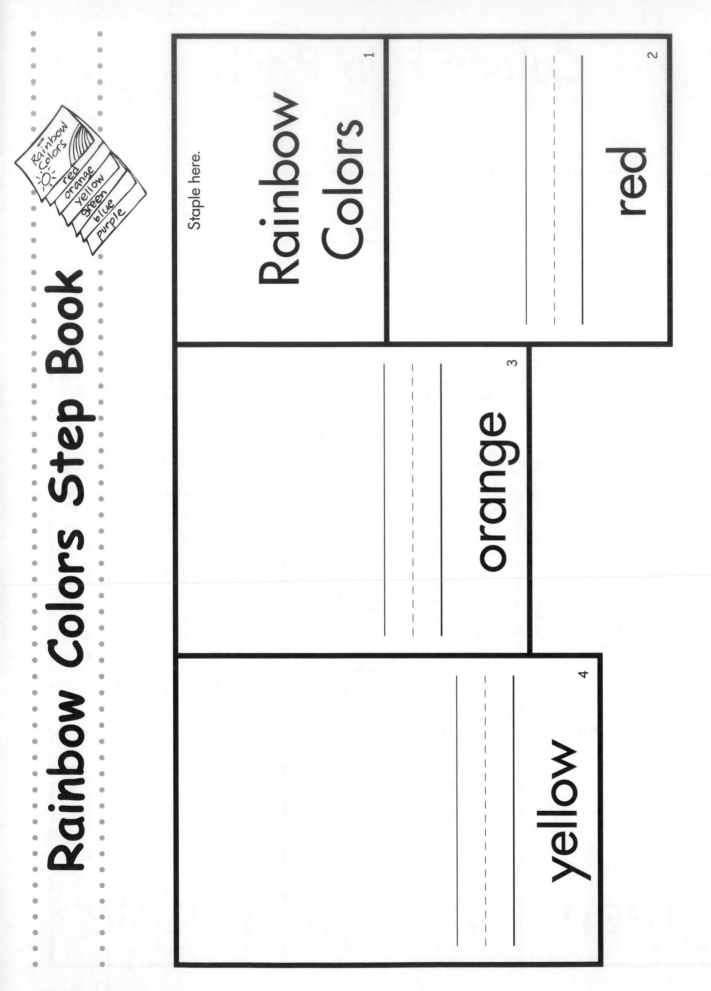

Staple here.

Rainbow Colors

1

red

2

orange

3

yellow

4

Build-a-Skill Instant Books • Color, Shape, and Number Words © 2015 Creative Teaching Press

green

5

blue

6

purple

7

Colors Flip Book

I can look at

Staple word cards here.

colors

blue
skies

brown
pies

yellow
fries

black
ties

green
guys

pink
butterflies

Colors Poem Strip Book

_____'s

Colors Poem

1

Orange is a carrot.
Yellow is a pear.

2

Green is the grass.

3

Colors Poem Strip Book

Brown is a bear.

4

Purple is a plum.

Blue is the sky.

5

Black is a funny hat.

Red is cherry pie.

6

Build-a-Skill Instant Books • Color, Shape, and Number Words © 2015 Creative Teaching Press

Staple word cards here.

I like

My favorite color is

I like red

My favorite color is red. Red is fun and happy. Red makes me smile.

Color Word Cards

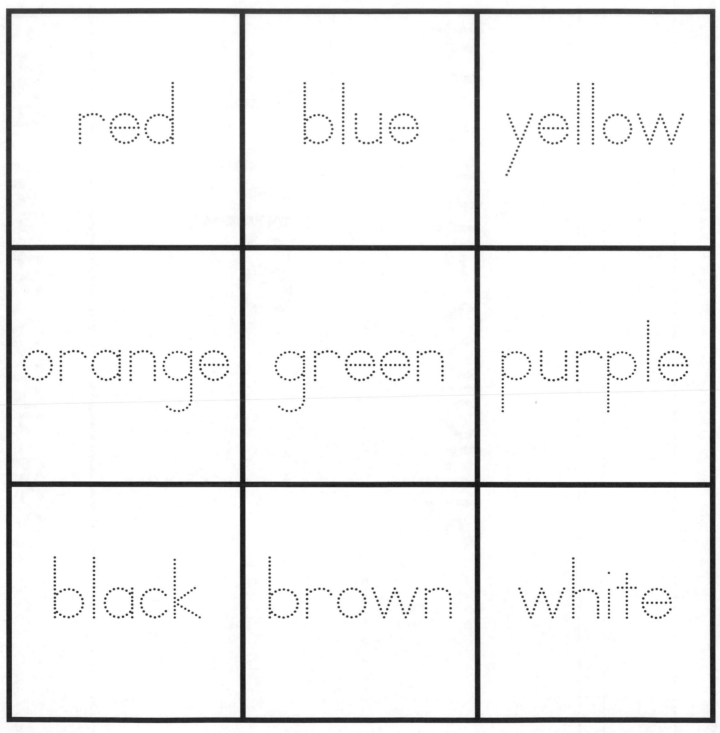

red	blue	yellow
orange	green	purple
black	brown	white

Build-a-Skill Instant Books • Color, Shape, and Number Words © 2015 Creative Teaching Press

Shapes Flip Book

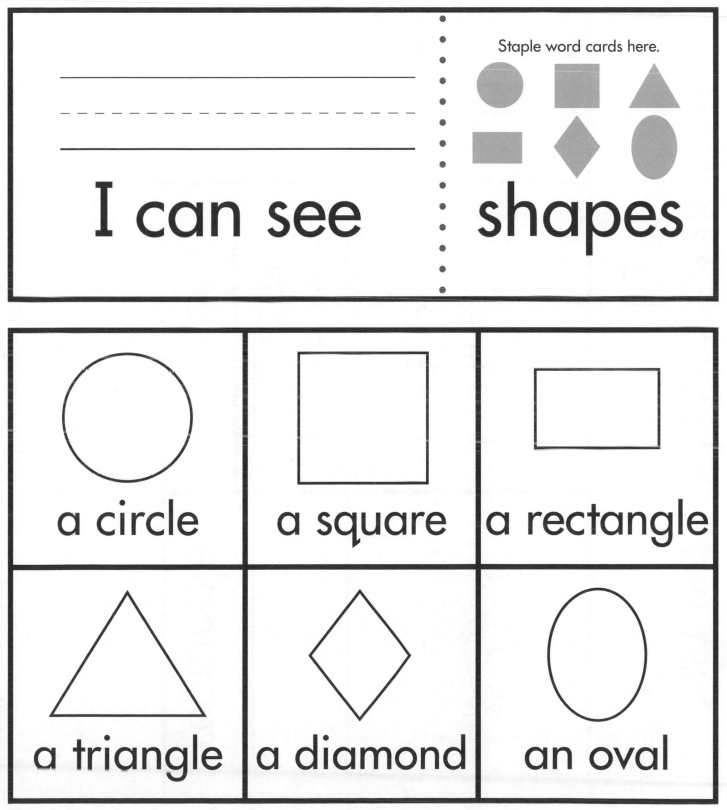

Staple word cards here.

I can see

shapes

a circle

a square

a rectangle

a triangle

a diamond

an oval

Fun with Shapes Step Book

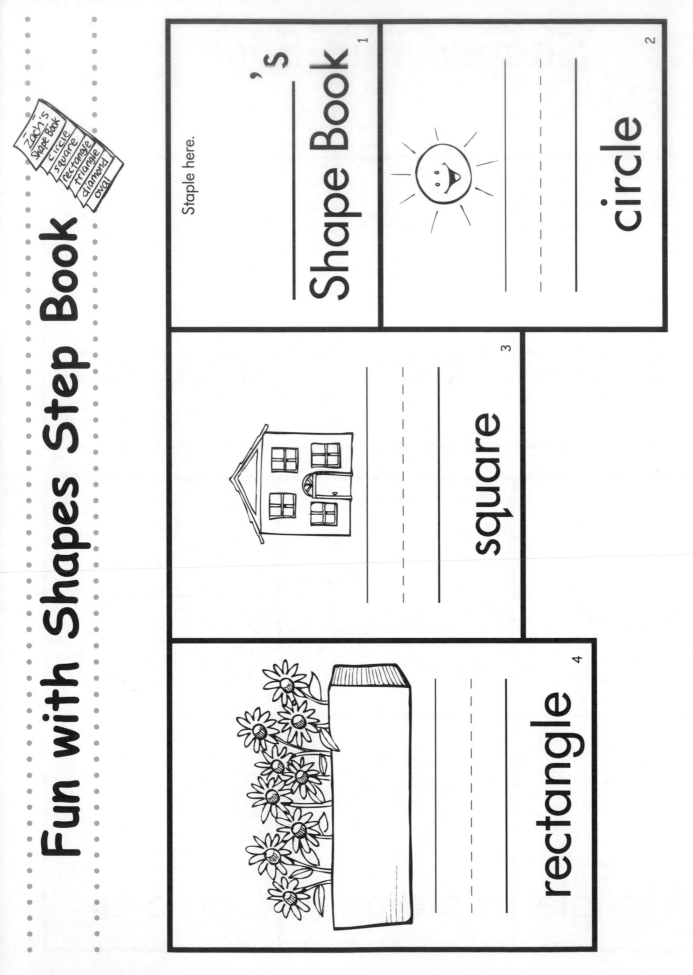

Staple here.

_____'s

Shape Book

1

_____

circle

2

_____

square

3

_____

rectangle

4

Build-a-Skill Instant Books • Color, Shape, and Number Words © 2015 Creative Teaching Press

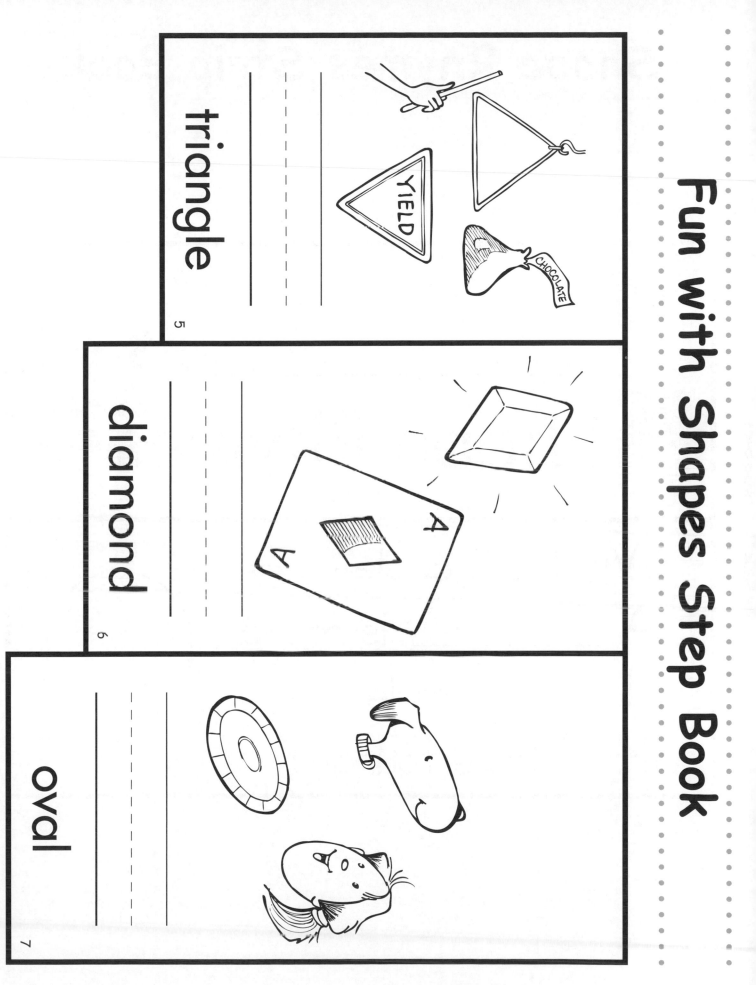

triangle

5

diamond

6

oval

7

Build-a-Skill Instant Books • Color, Shape, and Number Words © 2015 Creative Teaching Press

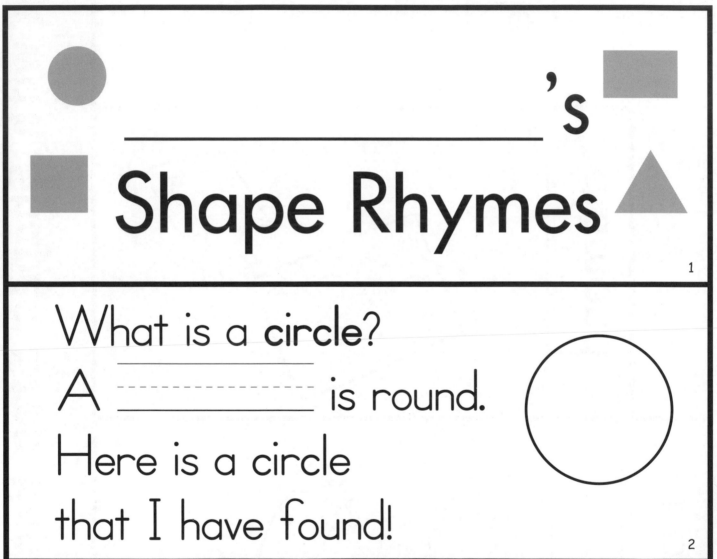

_____'s

Shape Rhymes

1

What is a **circle**?

A _____ is round.

Here is a circle
that I have found!

2

Build-a-Skill Instant Books • Color, Shape, and Number Words © 2015 Creative Teaching Press

Shape Rhymes Strip Book

What is a **triangle**?
Can you tell me?
A _____ has **3** sides;
Count them and see!

3

What is a **rectangle**?
It looks like a door.
A _____ has sides
1, 2, 3, 4!

4

What is a **square**?
A _____ has **4** sides, too.
But its sides are all equal,
that is your clue.

5

What Shape Is It? Mini Book

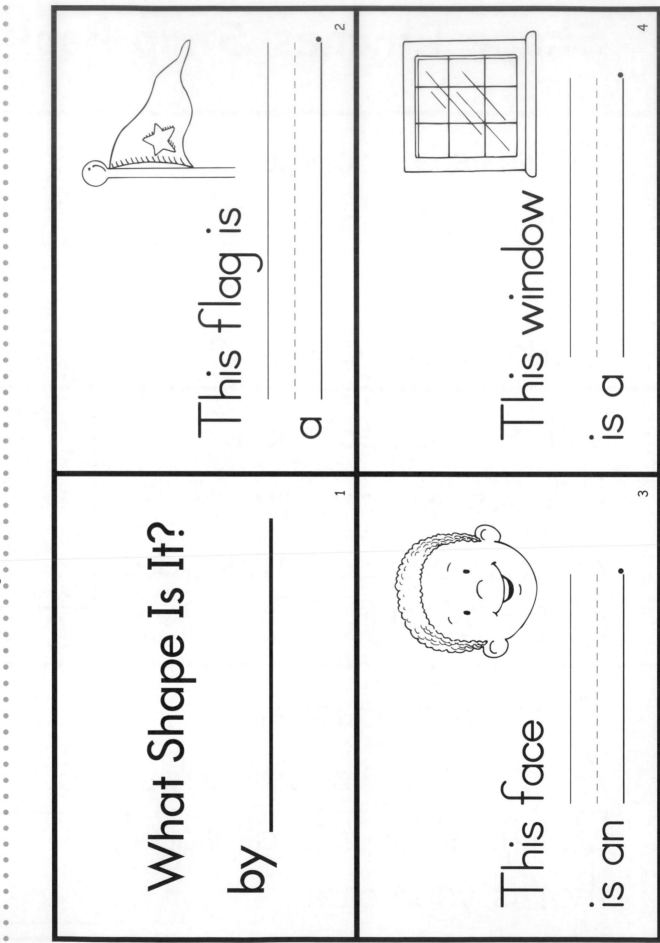

What Shape Is It?

by _____

1

This flag is _____

a

2

This face _____

is an

3

This window _____

is a

4

circle oval rectangle square diamond triangle

This kite is
a _____

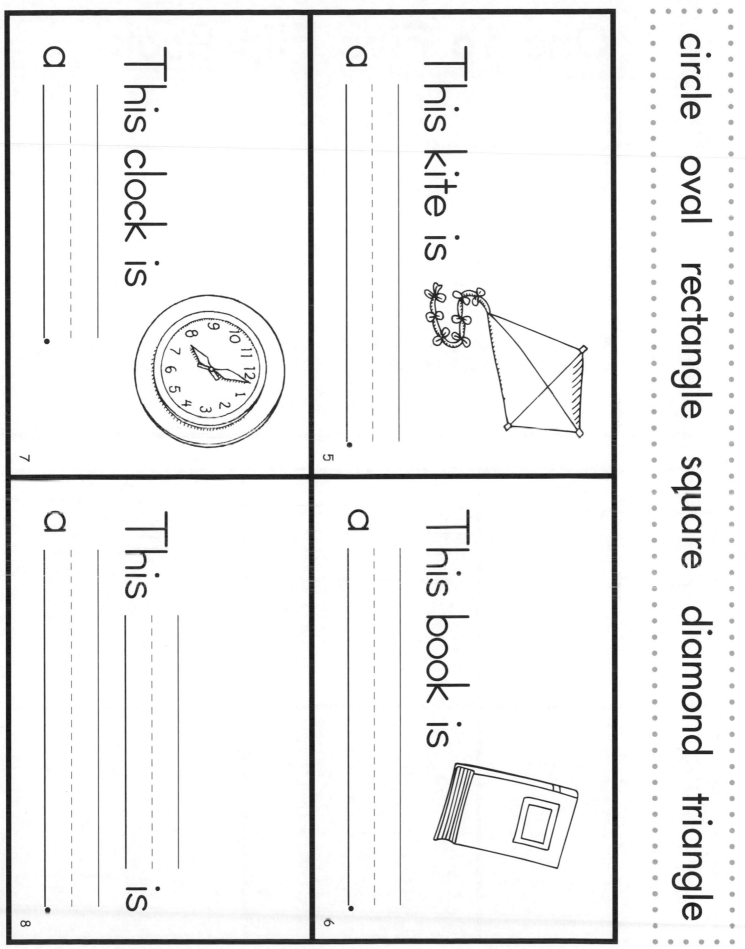

This book is
a _____

This clock is
a _____

This _____ is
a _____

Build-a-Skill Instant Books • Color, Shape, and Number Words © 2015 Creative Teaching Press

One to Five Flip Book

I can count

_____

- - - - - - - - - - - -

_____

I can count 1 2 3 4 5

Staple word cards here.

one

two

three

four

five

Build-a-Skill Instant Books • Color, Shape, and Number Words © 2015 Creative Teaching Press

Six to Ten Flip Book

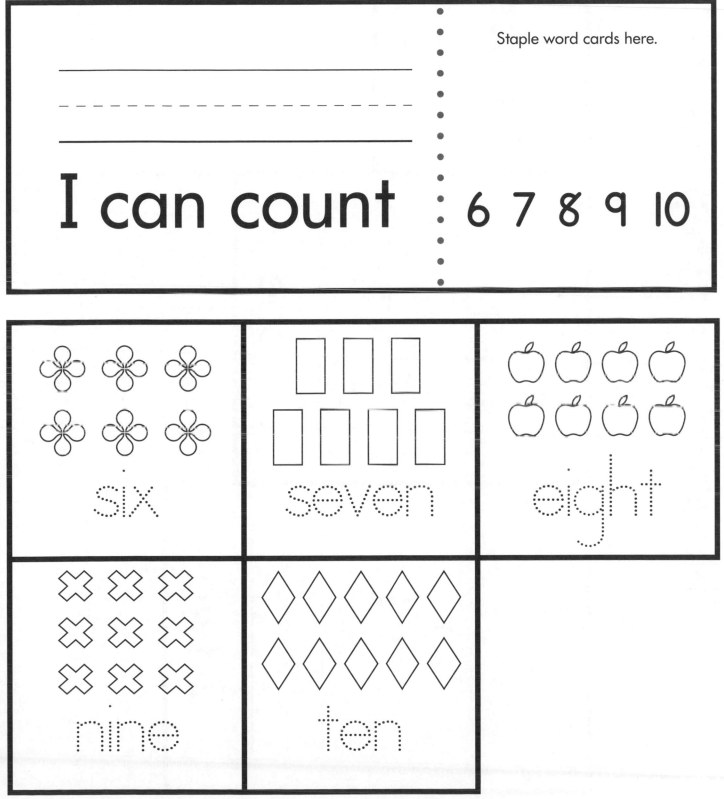

Staple word cards here.

I can count 6 7 8 9 10

six

seven

eight

nine

ten

Build-a-Skill Instant Books • Color, Shape, and Number Words © 2015 Creative Teaching Press

Number Fun Fun Step Book

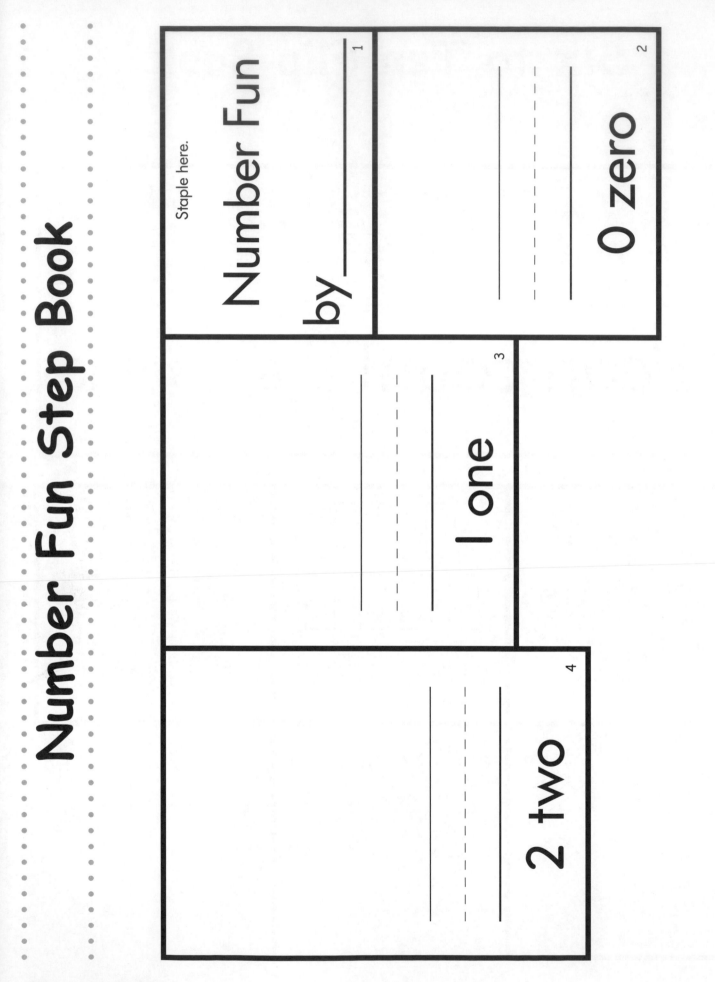

Staple here.

Number Fun

by _____

1

0 zero

2

I one

3

2 two

4

Build-a-Skill Instant Books • Color, Shape, and Number Words © 2015 Creative Teaching Press

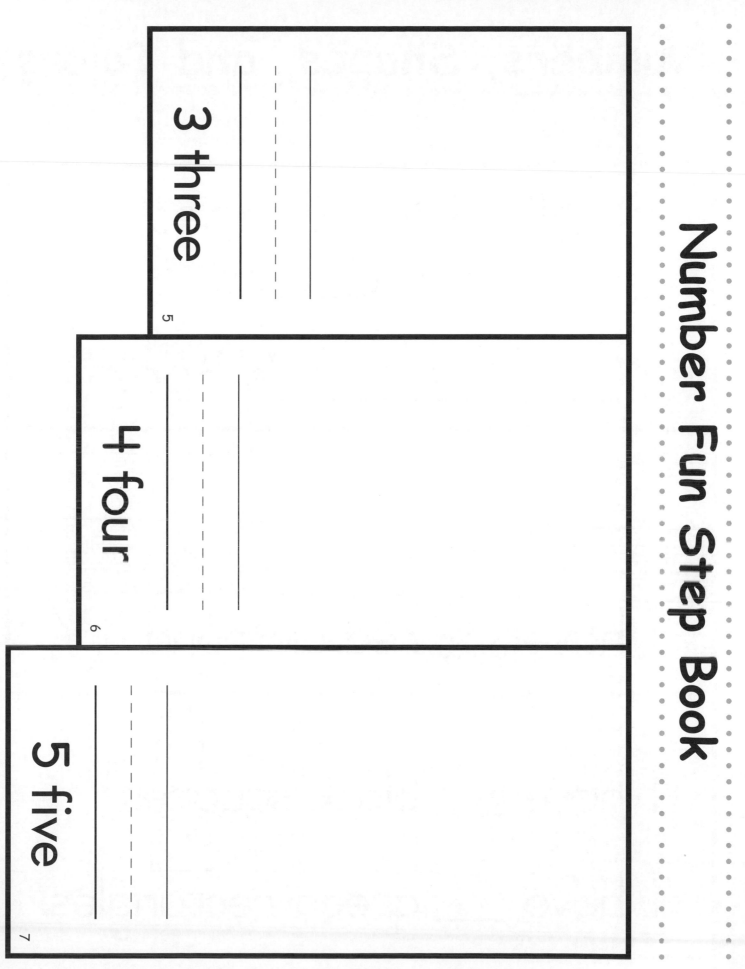

Number Fun Step Book

3 three

5

4 four

6

5 five

7

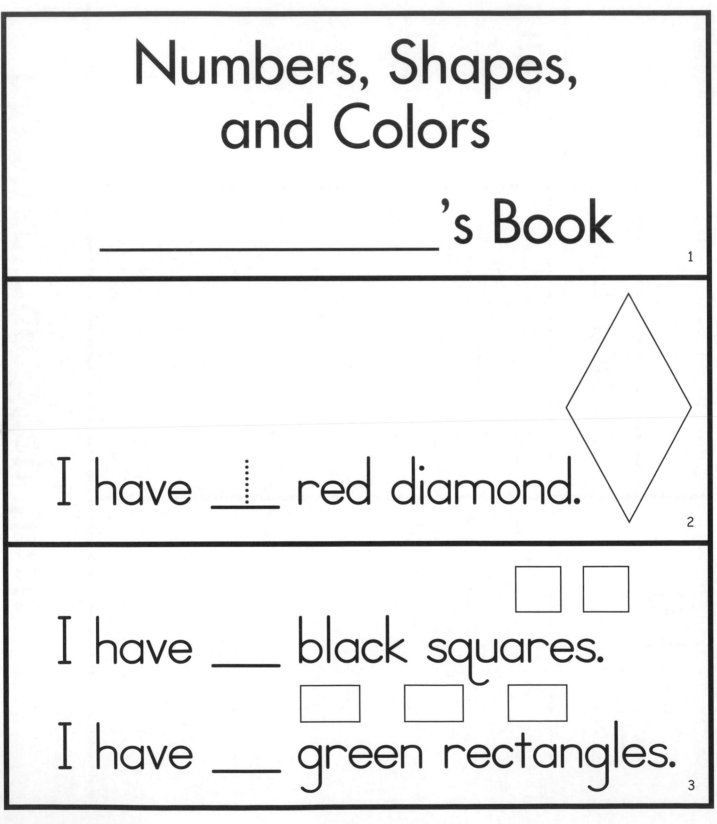

Numbers, Shapes,
and Colors

_____'s Book

1

I have __ red diamond.

2

I have __ black squares.

I have __ green rectangles.

3

Build-a-Skill Instant Books • Color, Shape, and Number Words © 2015 Creative Teaching Press

Numbers, Shapes, and Colors

I have ___ purple ovals.

I have ___ yellow triangles.

4

I have ___ pink circles.

5

I have ___ colorful butterfly.

6

I Spy Numbers and Colors

I Spy Numbers and Colors by _____

I spy _one_ yellow sun.

I spy _____ blue shoes.

I spy _____ green peas.

I spy _____ orange horns.

I spy _____ yellow hives.

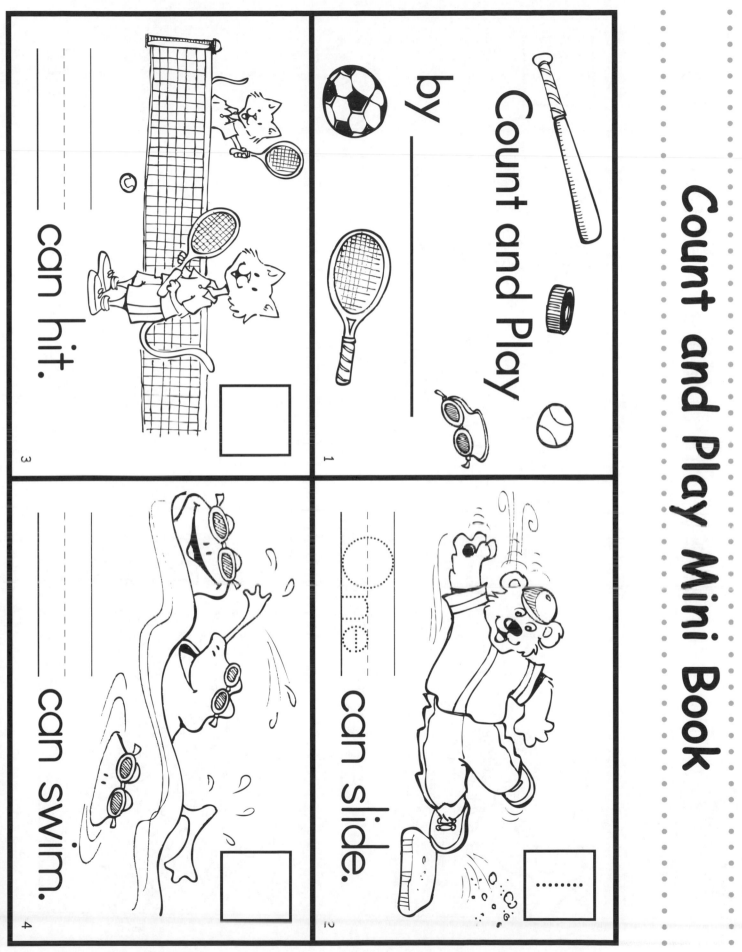

Count and Play

by

_____

_____

_____ can hit.

3

One can slide.

_____ can swim.

4

_____ can shoot.

6

We can all have fun!

8

_____ can skate.

5

_____ can run.

7

Build-a-Skill Instant Books • Color, Shape, and Number Words © 2015 Creative Teaching Press

Bug Countdown Strip Book

I see ten bugs in the garden.

1

I see nine bugs in the tree.

2

I see eight bugs on the sidewalk.

3

Bug Countdown Strip Book

I see seven bugs and one bee.

4

I see six bugs on the bed.

5

I see five bugs on the cat.

6

Build-a-Skill Instant Books • Color, Shape, and Number Words © 2015 Creative Teaching Press

Bug Countdown Strip Book

I see four bugs on the flower.
I see three bugs on the mat.

7

I see two bugs on the window.
I see one on the wall.

8

I see bugs everywhere,
and I can count them all!

9

Make Your Own Flip Book

Staple word cards here.

Build-a-Skill Instant Books • Color, Shape, and Number Words © 2015 Creative Teaching Press